OCEANS ALIVE

Seals

by Colleen Sexton

BELLWETHER MEDIA • MINNEAPOLIS, MN

Note to Librarians, Teachers, and Parents:

Blastoff! Readers are carefully developed by literacy experts and combine standards-based content with developmentally appropriate text.

Level 1 provides the most support through repetition of high-frequency words, light text, predictable sentence patterns, and strong visual support.

Level 2 offers early readers a bit more challenge through varied simple sentences, increased text load, and less repetition of high-frequency words.

Level 3 advances early-fluent readers toward fluency through increased text and concept load, less reliance on visuals, longer sentences, and more literary language.

Whichever book is right for your reader, Blastoff! Readers are the perfect books to build confidence and encourage a love of reading that will last a lifetime!

j 599.79
SEX
H gift 4/4/08

This edition first published in 2007 by Bellwether Media.

No part of this publication may be reproduced in whole or in part without written permission of the publisher. For information regarding permission, write to Bellwether Media Inc., Attention: Permissions Department, Post Office Box 1C, Minnetonka, MN 55345-9998.

Library of Congress Cataloging-in-Publication Data
Sexton, Colleen A.
  Seals / by Colleen Sexton.
    p. cm. — (Oceans alive)
Summary: "Simple text and supportive full-color photographs introduce beginning readers to seals. Intended for kindergarten through third grade students"—Provided by publisher.
  Includes bibliographical references and index.
  ISBN-13: 978-1-60014-056-3 (hardcover : alk. paper)
  ISBN-10: 1-60014-056-4 (hardcover : alk. paper)
  1. Seals (Animals)—Juvenile literature. I. Title.

QL737.P63S47 2007
599.79—dc22   2006035211

Contents

Most seals live along the **ocean** shore. Some seals live near rocky places.

4

Some seals live near
icy places.

Ringed seals are the smallest
kind of seal. They are smaller
than an adult man.

Elephant seals are the biggest kind of seal. They can be bigger than a car.

Seals have fat called **blubber** under their skin.

Blubber keeps seals warm
in cold water and on ice.

Thick fur keeps seals warm
too. Most seals have brown,
gray, or silver fur.

10

Some seals have spots. These spots help seals **blend** in with the shore.

Seals have big, round eyes.

whiskers

Seals have long **whiskers**.
Seals use their whiskers to
feel things.

flippers

Seals have two front **flippers**.
The front flippers are short
and have claws.

flippers

Seals have two back flippers. They move their back flippers up and down to swim.

15

Seals are fast swimmers.
They twist and glide in
the water.

Seals can **dive** deep into the ocean.

Seals hunt for food in the ocean. Seals eat fish, shrimp, crabs, and squid.

Seals are slow on land.
They flop on their bellies
to move.

Seals live in groups.

They rest together in the sun.

Glossary

blend—when something looks so much like the things around it that it becomes hard to see

blubber—a thick layer of fat just under the skin; most seals live in cold places and need blubber to keep warm.

dive—to rush head first into the water; seals dive deep and can hold their breath for 20 minutes or longer.

elephant seal—the biggest kind of seal; the elephant seal lives near ocean shores in parts of North America, South America, Africa, and Australia.

flipper—a wide, flat limb that some ocean animals use to swim; seals have webbed "fingers" at the ends of their flippers.

ocean—a large body of salty water; seals live at the edge of the ocean on the land or ice and in the water.

ringed seal—the smallest kind of seal; ringed seals live near the Arctic.

whiskers—stiff hairs that grow near an animal's mouth; seals can feel their surroundings with their whiskers.

To Learn More

AT THE LIBRARY

Hodgkins, Fran. *The Orphan Seal*. Camden, Maine: Down East Books, 2000.

Hollenbeck, Kathleen M. *Islands of Ice: The Story of a Harp Seal*. Norwalk, Conn.: Soundprints, 2001.

Kalman, Bobbie. *Seals and Sea Lions*. New York: Crabtree Publishing, 2006.

Stille, Darlene. *I Am a Seal: The Life of an Elephant Seal*. Minneapolis: Picture Window Books, 2005.

Zoehfeld, Kathleen Weidner. *Seal Pup Grows Up: The Story of a Harbor Seal*. Norwalk, Conn.: Soundprints, 1994.

ON THE WEB
Learning more about seals is as easy as 1, 2, 3.

1. Go to www.factsurfer.com

2. Enter "seals" into search box.

3. Click the "Surf" button and you will see a list of related web sites.

With factsurfer.com, finding more information is just a click away.

Index

The photographs in this book are reproduced through the courtesy of: James D. Watt/image-questmarine.com, front cover; Konstantinas, p. 4; Kevin Schafer/Getty Images, p. 5; David Hosking/Getty Images, p. 6; James D. Watt/imagequestmarine.com, p. 7; Pascaline Daniel, pp. 8-9; Masa Ushioda/imagequestmarine.com, p. 10; Trout55, p. 11; CoverStock, p. 12, Sebastien Burel, p. 13; Tim Zurowski, pp. 14-15; Klaus Jost/imagequestmarine.com, pp. 16-17, 20-21; Brian J. Skerry/Getty Images, p. 18; The Image Bank/Getty Iamges, p. 19.